Christian JOKES

for

EVERYONE

150 Clean and Funny Christian Jokes/ Riddles

HA HA HA HA

HA HA HA HA

Who was the first drug addict in the Bible?

Nebuchadnezzar. He was on grass for seven years.

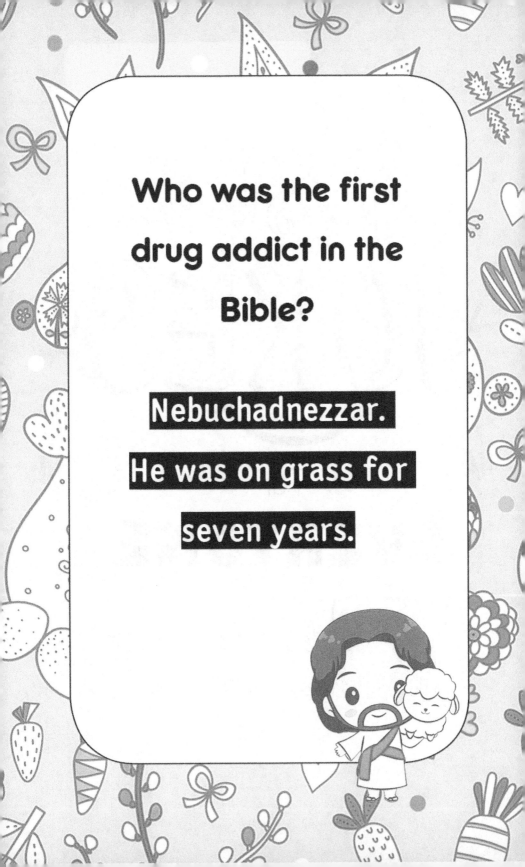

Will there be dogs in the new system?

No, 2 Peter 3:14 tells us that we will be without spot.

Who was the straightest man in the bible?

Joseph, because the Pharaoh made him a ruler.

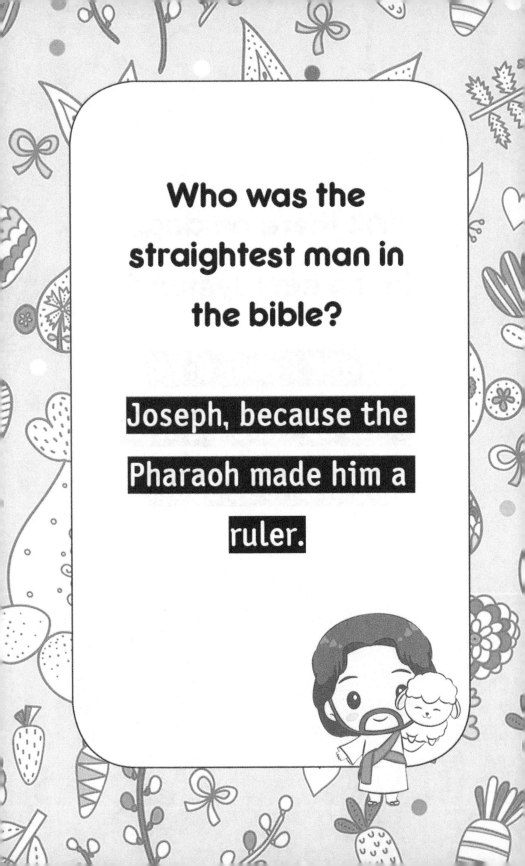

Which Christian magazine did the apostle Paul command to never throw away?

Ephesians 5:18 says to "keep Awake"

What kind of motor vehicles are in the Bible?

Jehovah drove Adam and Eve out of the Garden in a Fury.

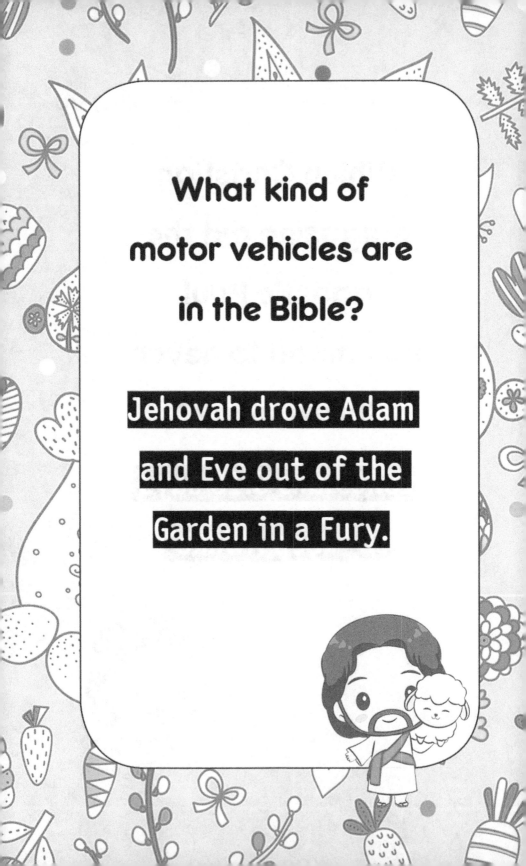

I am the greatest financier in the Bible. I floated my stock while everyone was in liquidation. Who am I?

Noah. He was floating his stock while everyone else was in liquidation.

What kind of motor vehicles are in the Bible?

David's Triumph was heard throughout the land.

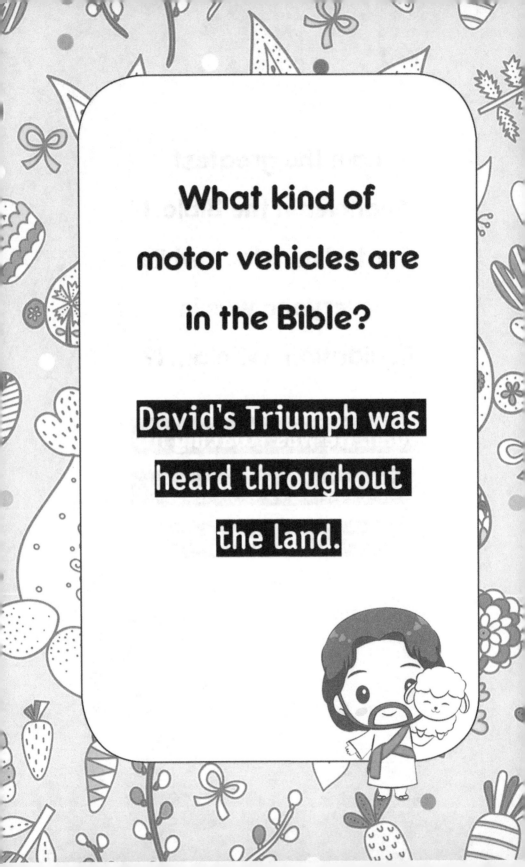

What kind of motor vehicles are in the Bible?

Honda...because the apostles were all in one Accord.

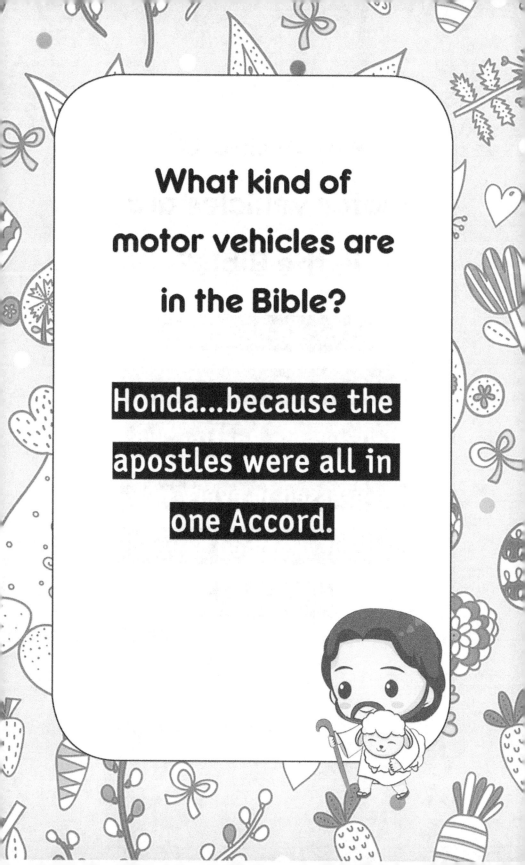

What kind of motor vehicles are in the Bible?

2 Cor. 48 describes going out in service in a Volkswagen Beetle: "We are pressed in every way, but not cramped beyond movement."

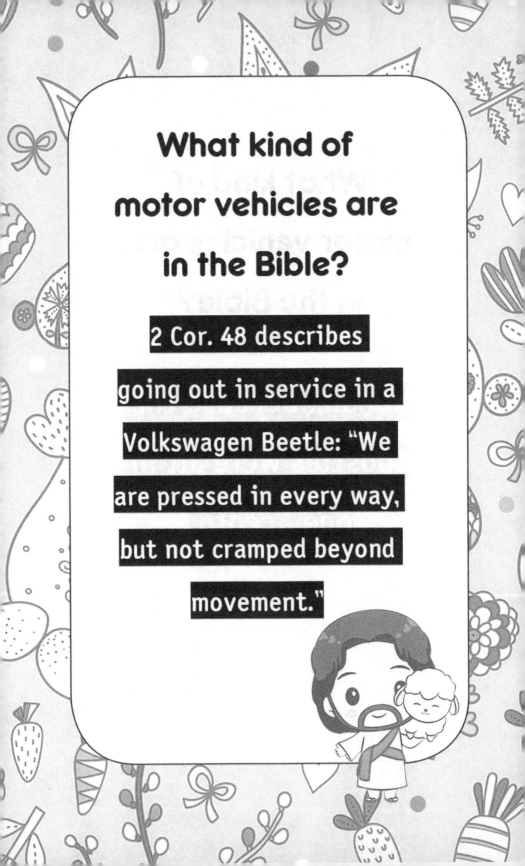

What do they call pastors in Germany?

German Shepherds.

What is the best way to get to Paradise?

Turn right and go straight.

Where is the first tennis match mentioned in the Bible?

When Joseph served in Pharaoh's court.

When was the longest day in the Bible?

The day Adam was created because there was no Eve.

What excuse did Adam give to his children as to why he no longer lived in Eden?

Your mother ate us out of house and home.

Why didn't they play cards on the Ark?

Because Noah was standing on the deck.

Why couldn't Jonah trust the ocean?

Because he knew there was something fishy about it.

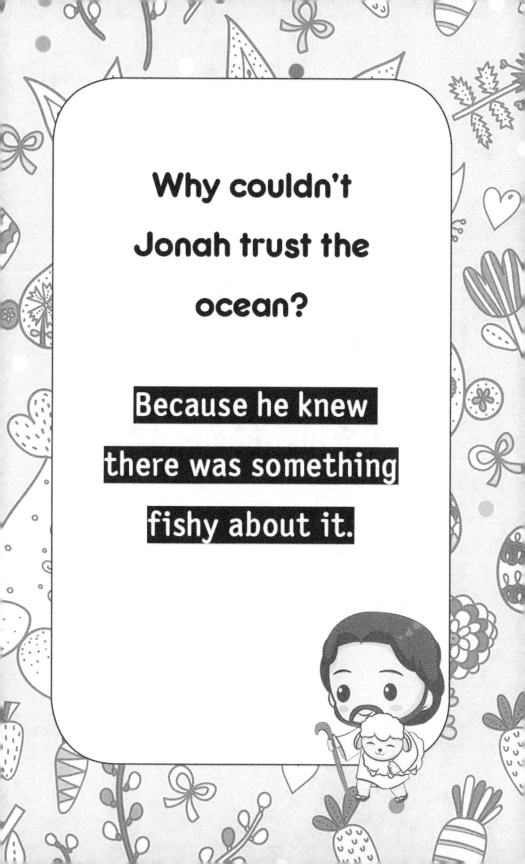

Did Eve ever have a date with Adam?

No, just an apple.

Where was Solomon's temple located?

On the side of his head.

Why didn't Noah go fishing?

He only had two worms.

What did Adam say on the day before Christmas?

It's Christmas, Eve!

How does Moses
make his coffee?

Hebrews it.

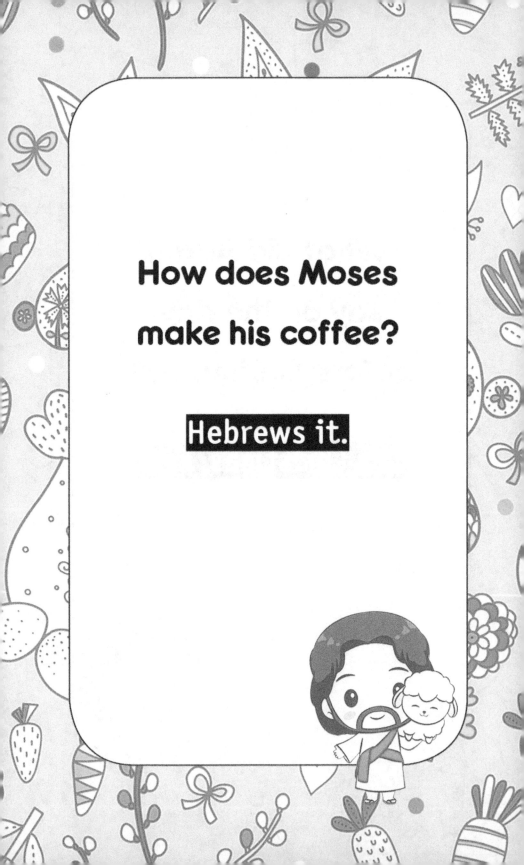

How do we know
Peter was a rich
fisherman?

By his net income.

Who were Gumby's favorite Bible characters?

Shadrack, Meshack & AhBENDago.

Who was the smartest man in the Bible?

Abraham. He knew a Lot.

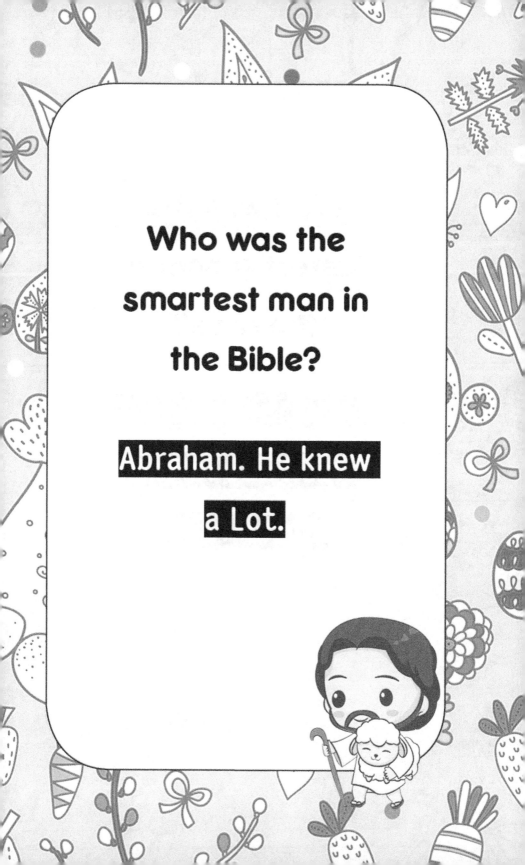

Who was the fastest runner in the race?

Adam, because he was first in the human race.

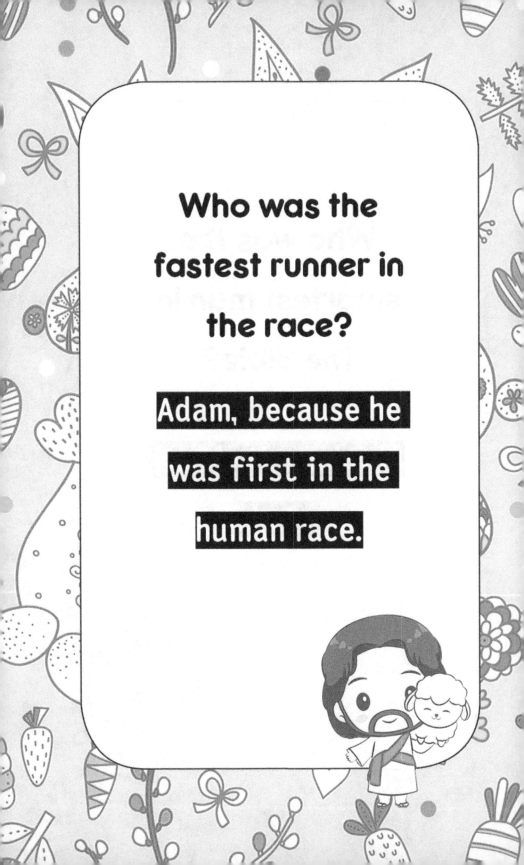

Why did the unemployed man get excited while looking through his Bible?

He thought he saw a job.

What animal could Noah not trust?

Cheetah

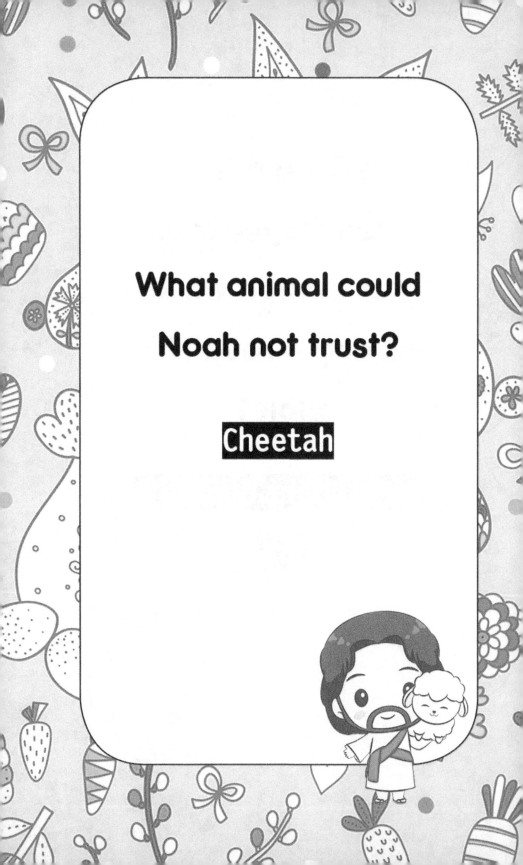

Who was the greatest comedian in the Bible?

Samson. He brought the house down.

What kind of man
was Boaz before
he married?

Ruthless.

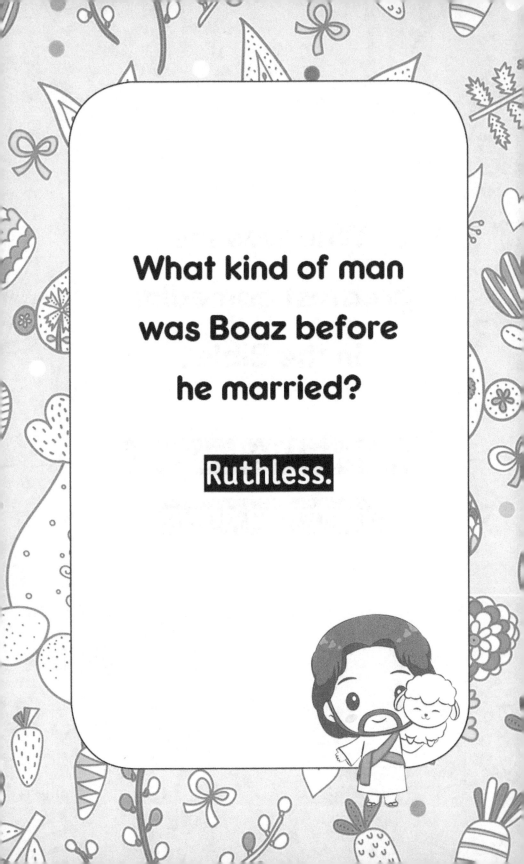

On the Ark, Noah probably got milk from the cows. What did he get from the ducks?

Quackers.

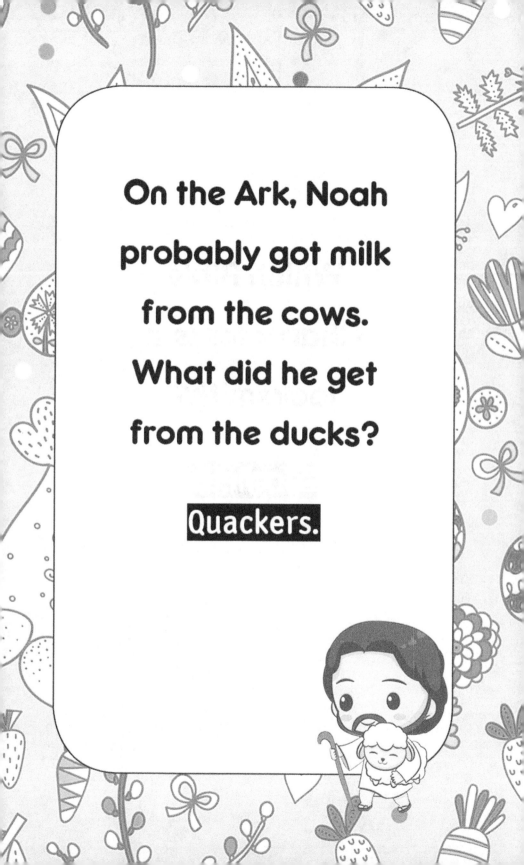

Which Bible
Character is a
locksmith?

Zaccheus

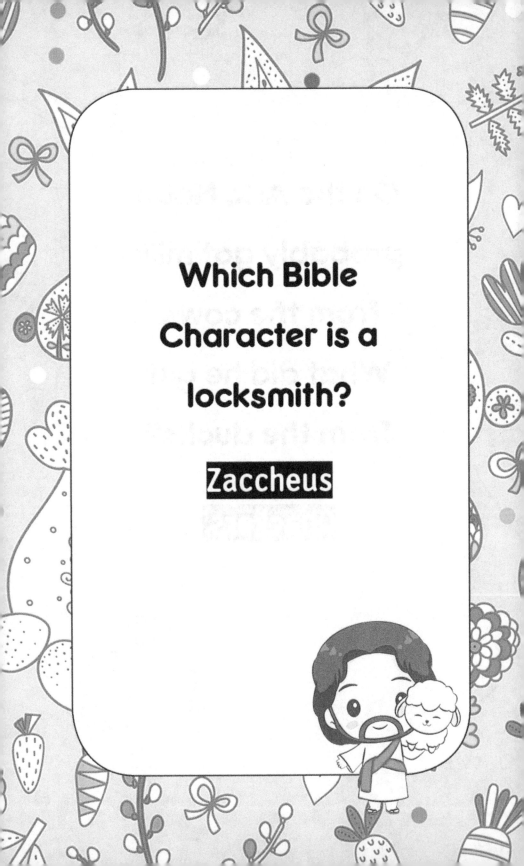

Which Bible character had no parents?

Joshua, son of Nun

Where is the first baseball game in the Bible?

In the big inning. Eve stole first, Adam stole second. Cain struck out Abel. The Giants and the Angels were rained out.

What's a dentist's favorite hymn?

Crown him with many crowns.

What kind of car
does Jesus
typically drive?

A Christler.

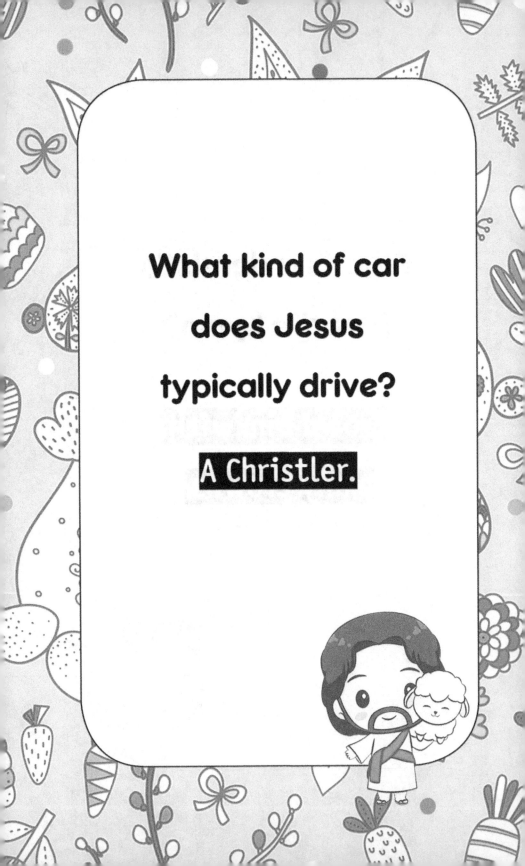

Did you know baseball was mentioned in the Bible?

It starts off "In the big inning

What kind of man
was Boaz before
he got married?

He was Ruth-less.

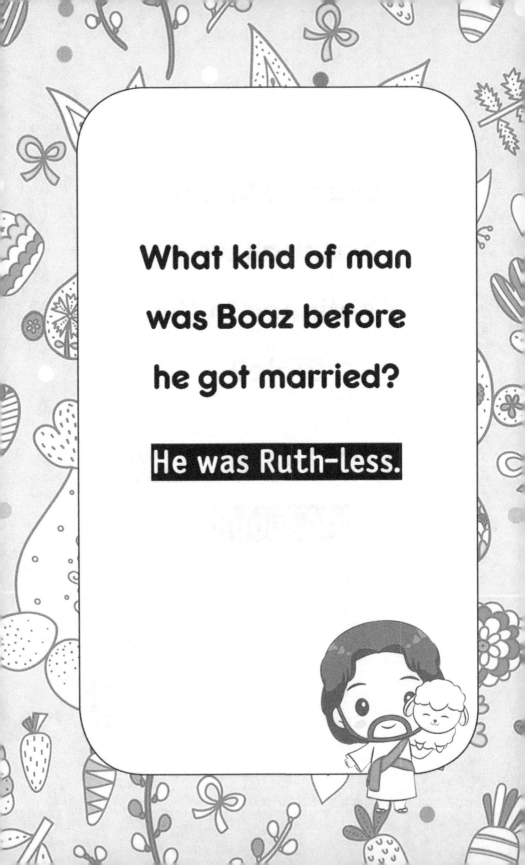

If Goliath would come back to life today, would you like to tell him the joke about David and Goliath?

No, he already fell for it once.

What's a missionary's favorite type of car?

A convertible. Yo mamma so old she pre-order the Bible. (oh snap!)

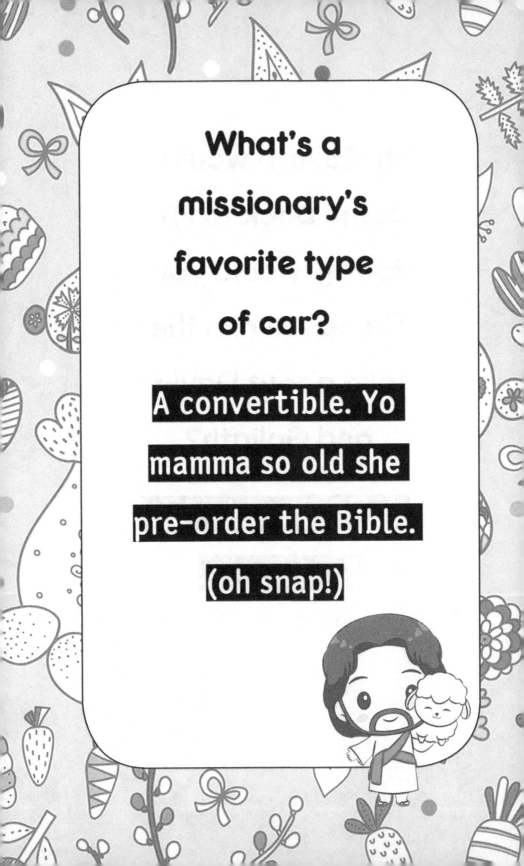

Why is it a bad idea to fart in church?

You have to sit in your own "pew"

When was the first math homework problem mentioned in the Bible?

When God told Adam and Eve to go forth and multiply.

Why did Noah have to punish and discipline the chickens on the Ark?

They were using fowl language.

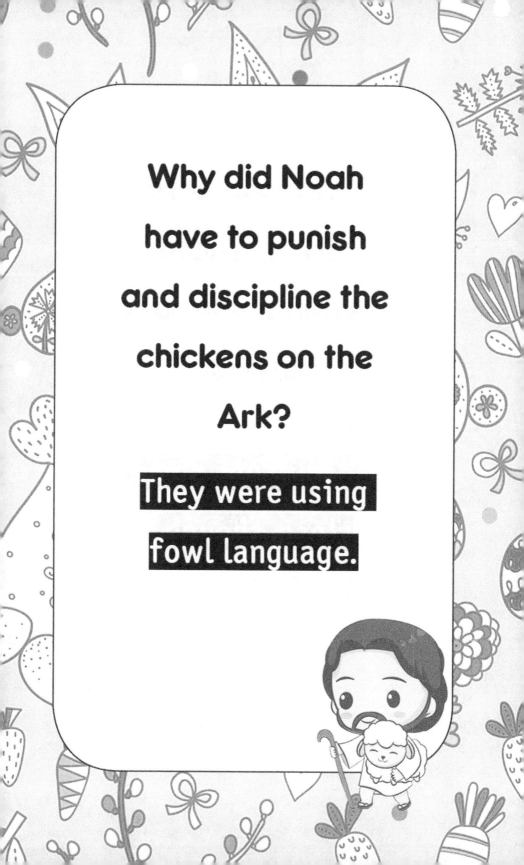

The good Lord
didn't create
anything without a
purpose

Mosquitoes come
close, though.

What do donkeys send out near Christmas?

Mule-tide greetings.

Which area of Palestine was especially wealthy?

The area around the River Jordan. The banks were always overflowing.

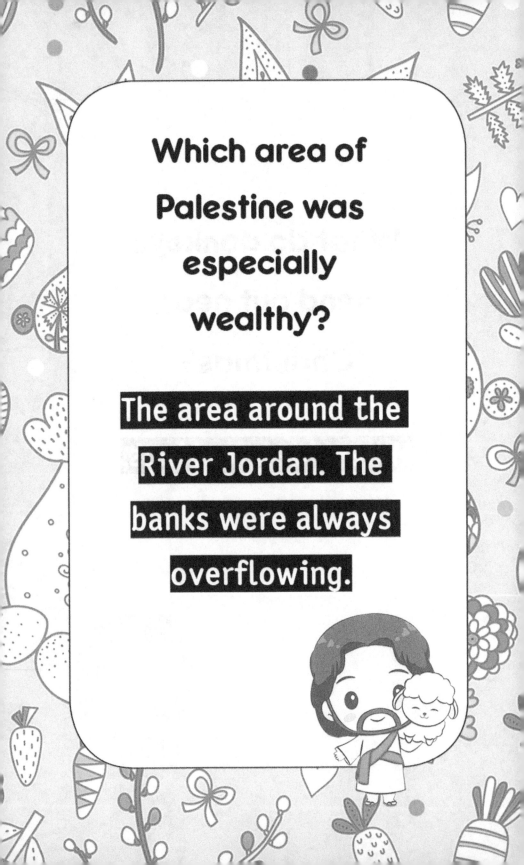

Where is medicine first mentioned in the Bible?

When God gave Moses two tablets.

How many people can you fit in one Honda?

Well, the Bible said that all 12 disciples were in one Accord.

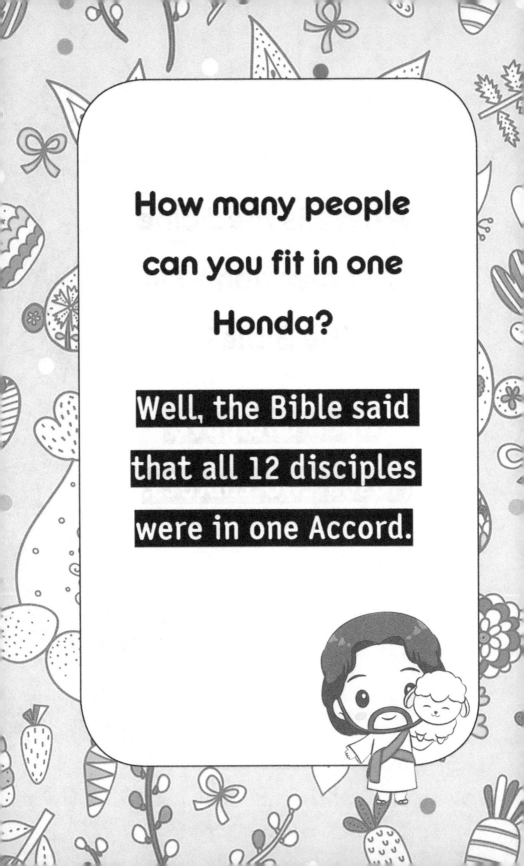

What was the first
word out of
Adam's mouth
when he first saw
Eve?

Whoa man! Thus, the
word "woman" was
created.

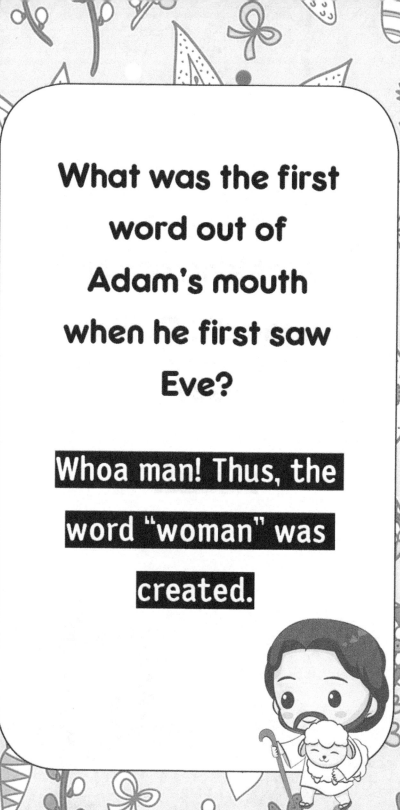

What kind of cell phone did Delilah use?

Samson

Who do mice pray to?

Cheesus.

You might see this in
the sky
By a waterfall its lower
Some say that it was
first seen
After a flood by Noah

A rainbow

He led Israelites out of
Egypt
And went up Mount Sinai
alone
He came back down with
ten commandments
Written on two tablets of
stone
Who is this man?

Moses

It had so many locks that don't need a key. It was far too many for you to count. It was never to be shortened, for a vow had been said. It was a symbol of strength that flowed from the head. But in a moment of weakness, its secret was out, it lays all in pieces when she gave the shout. What is it?

Samson's long hair

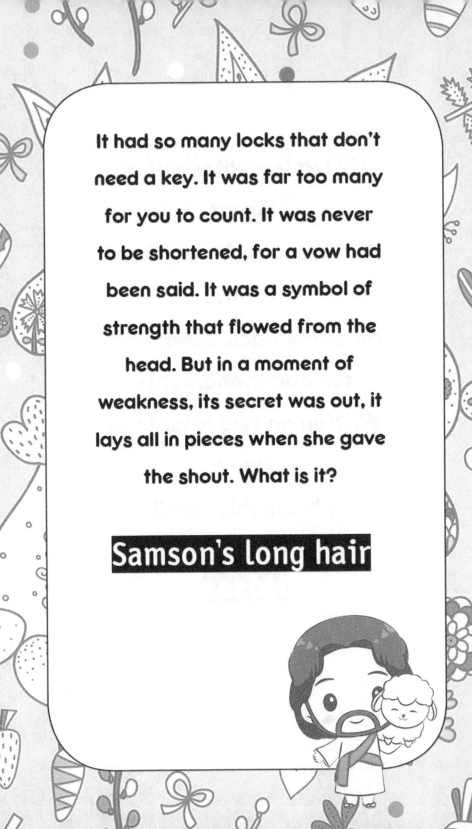

From my shoulders and upward, I was higher than any of the people? Who am I?

Saul

I look like the letter T and Am a symbol of Christianity. What is it?

The Cross

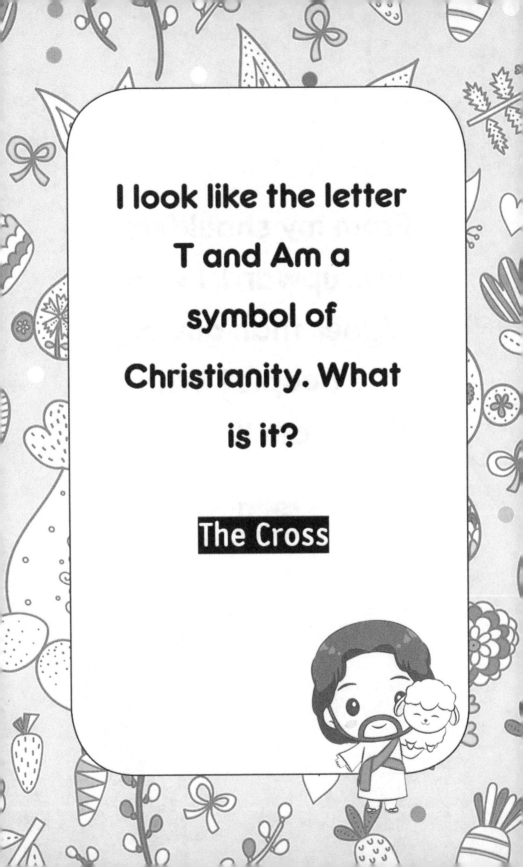

It's not a person
nor an animal but
He's got a face.
Who is he?

God

I kept him steady and others
away
I kept them safe and showed
the way
Once thrown down upon the
ground
I came alive with a hissing
sound
I hit the rock as he was told
And that was when the water
flowed
What am I?

Moses' Staff

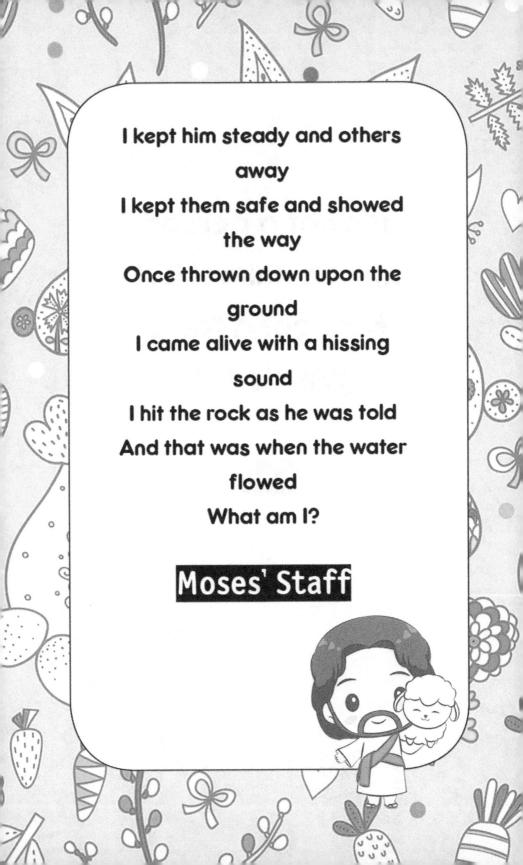

How long did Cain hate his brother?

As long as he was Abel.

I can be carried but not touched
I have two on the outside and ten on the inside
Everyone wants to catch a sight of me
But I'm kept out of sight
I was lost and found; then found but now I am lost
I'm in the Bible – what am I?

The Ark of the Covenant

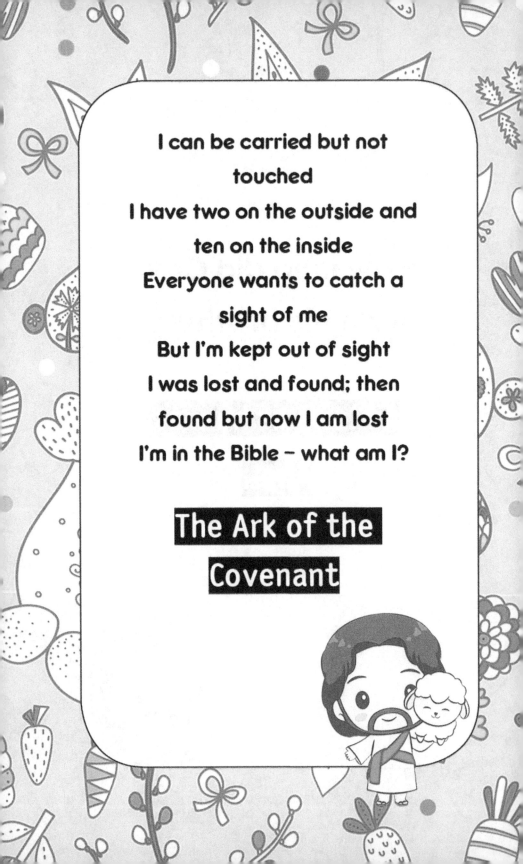

Why did Eve want to leave the Garden of Eden and move to New York?

She fell for the Big Apple

There was a man who went one day

On top a Joppa house to pray,

And while he waited for his meat

He dreamed he saw a great big

sheet

Let down from heaven, and inside

Fowls and creeping things did ride,

The one who prayed was told to eat,

For God had cleansed this

"common" meat.

Who was he?

Peter

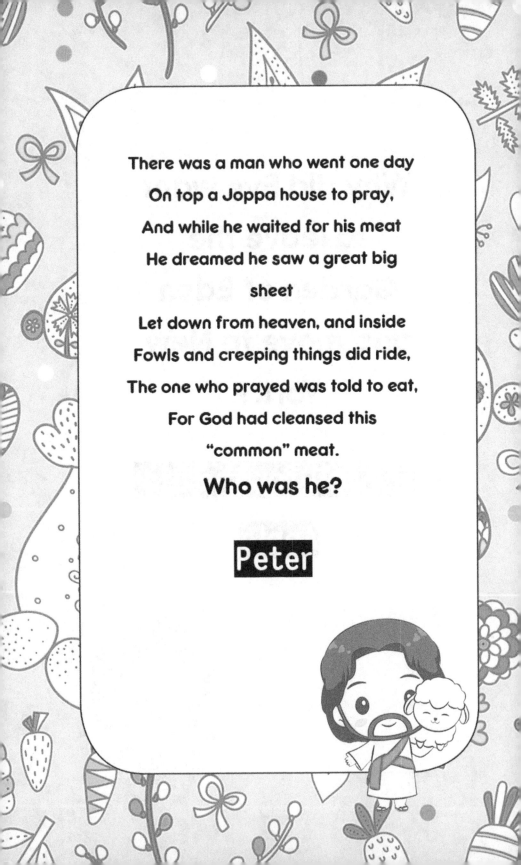

I was the king who was encouraged by the queen when I was greatly troubled by writing on the wall.

Who am I?

Belshazzar

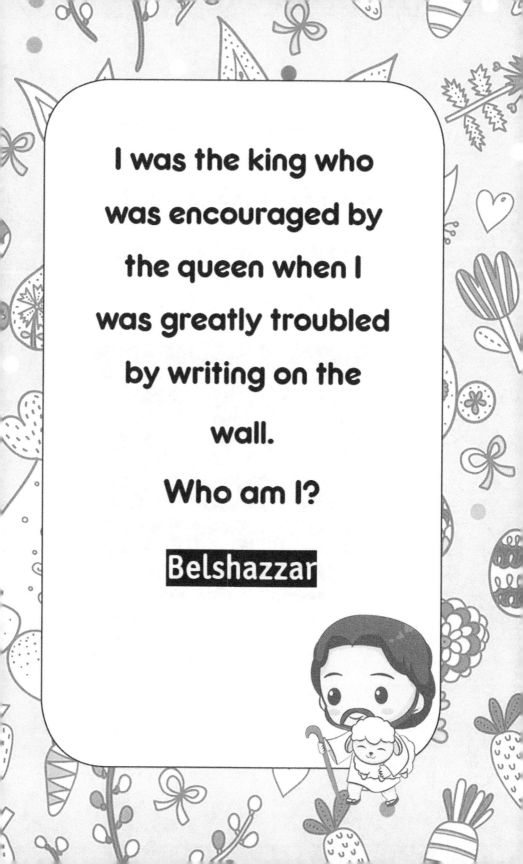

It is greater than God and more evil than the devil. The poor have it, the rich need it and if you eat it you'll die.

What is it?

Nothing. Nothing is greater than God, nothing is eviler than the devil, the poor have nothing, the rich need nothing, and if you eat nothing you will die.

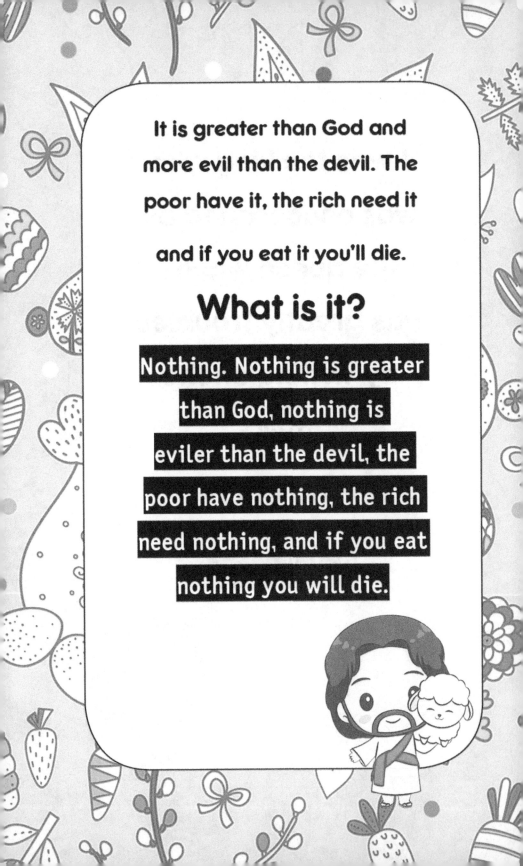

Why did Samson try to avoid arguing with Delilah?

He didn't want to split hairs

What sort of lights were on Noah's Ark?

Flood lights.

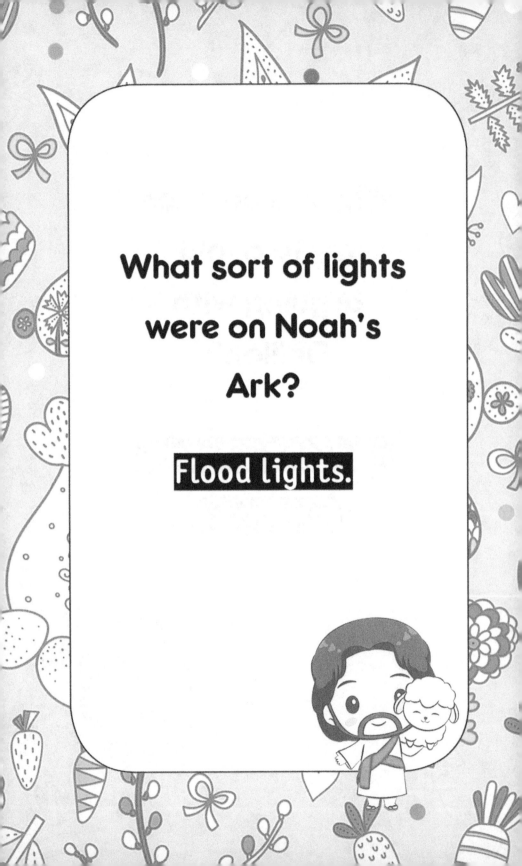

Need an Ark built?

I Noah guy.

Why wouldn't the Pharaoh let the Hebrews go?

He was in 'de Nile.

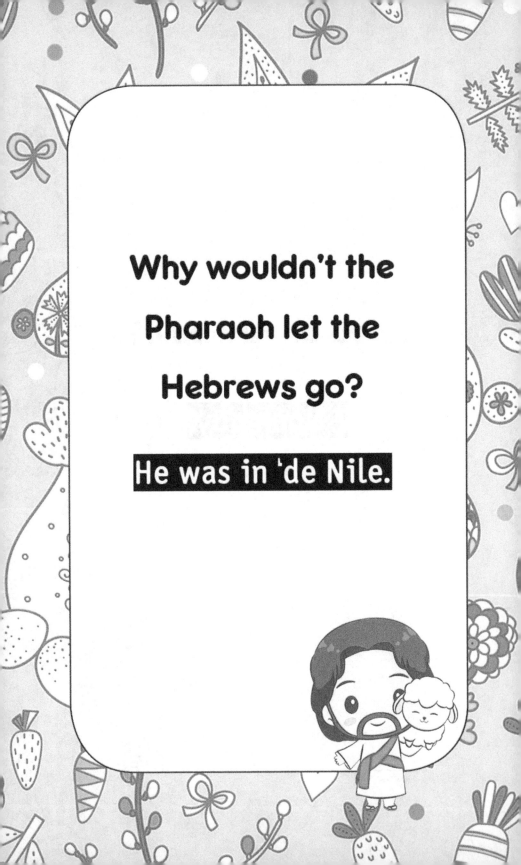

What's a salesman's favorite Scripture passage?

The Great Commission.

Which biblical character was the youngest to speak foul language?

Job, because he cursed the day he was born.

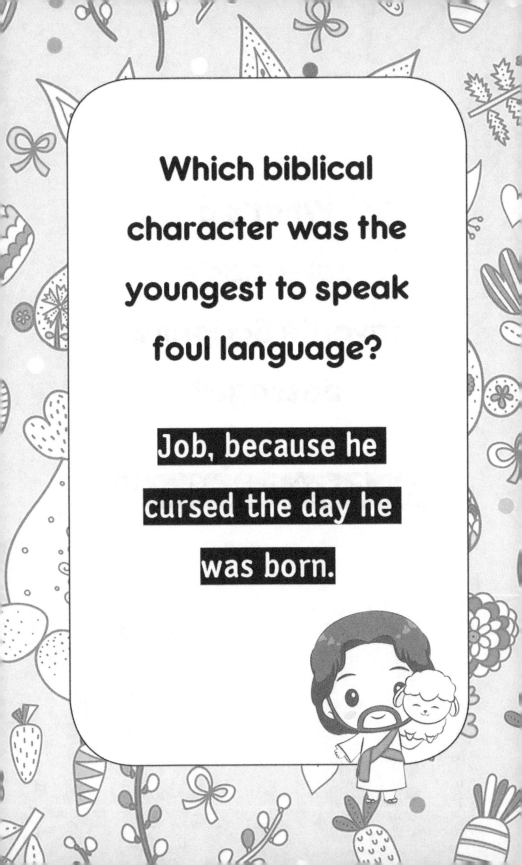

Why did the hawk sit on the church steeple?

Because it was a bird of pray.

What is the most religious cheese?

Swiss, because it's holy.

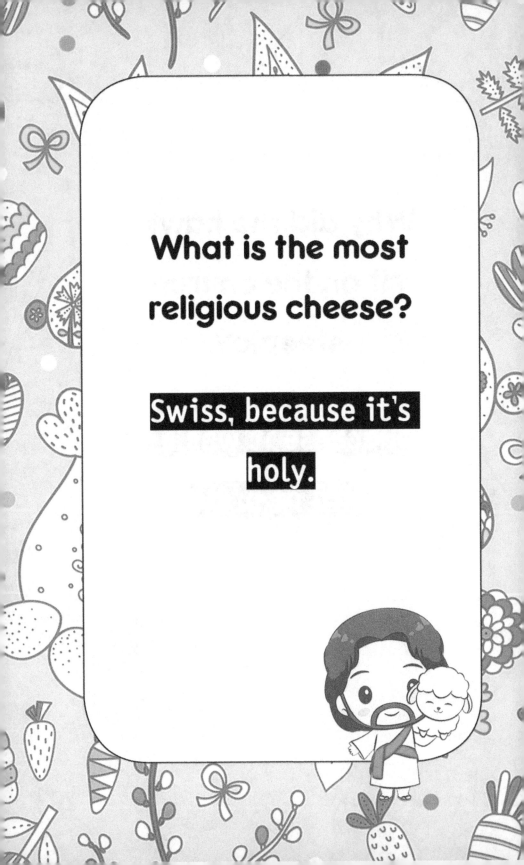

What's the best way to settle church disputes?

With canons.

Who's the patron saint of poverty?

St. Nickeless.

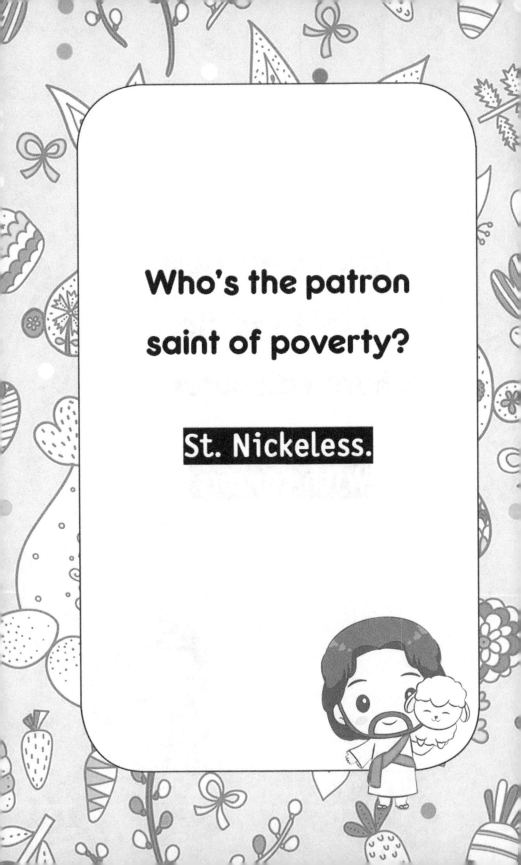

I didn't have faith
when I was walking
on the water.

Peter

I wrote Paul's letter to the Romans.

Tertius

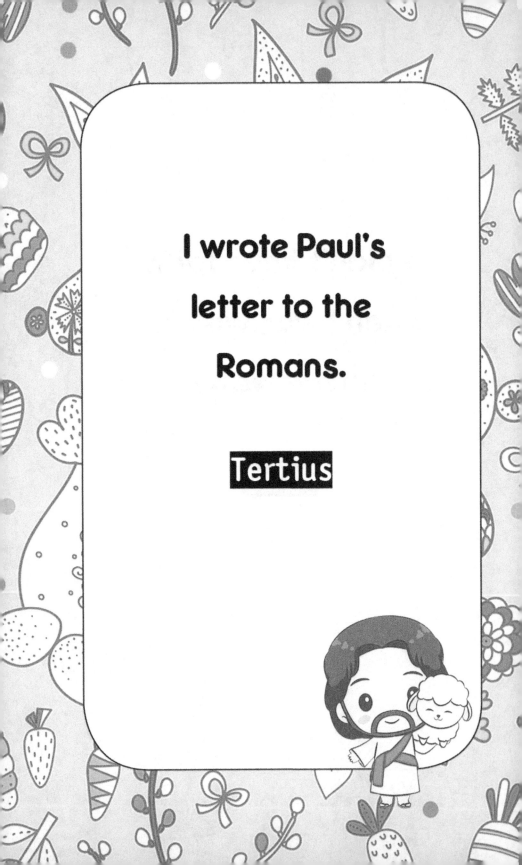

I was a judge. I fell backward from my seat and died.

Eli.

I am a creature without legs and a tongue that has a fork. You might hear parseltongue if you found one that could talk.

What am I?

A snake

On his arc, how many of each animal did Moses bring?

None. Because Moses did not have an arc, Noah did.

What did the High Priest say before he went to flush the toilet?

Holy crap!

I can look like a T, I can look like an X. I can be found on chains, hung around people's necks. What am I?

A cross

What is the best possible way to study the Bible?

You Luke into it.

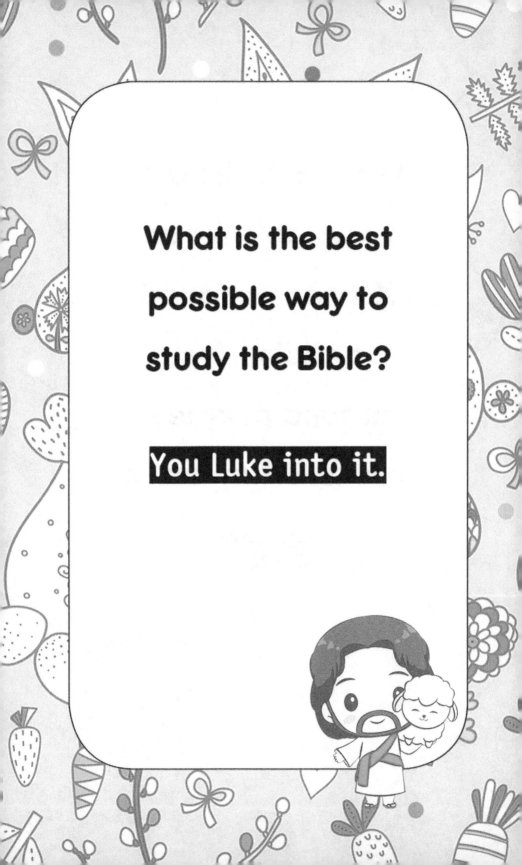

I may seem like a strange mix but I'm there for all to see. With parents, shepherds and kings, some animals, and a baby. What am I?

Nativity scene.

It was a gift to the one but poison to the others. It was a favored sign but also a hated symbol. Some say that It was not short. While others talk of two that were far too long. It was stolen and then torn, and became something to mourn.

What is it?

Joseph's coat.

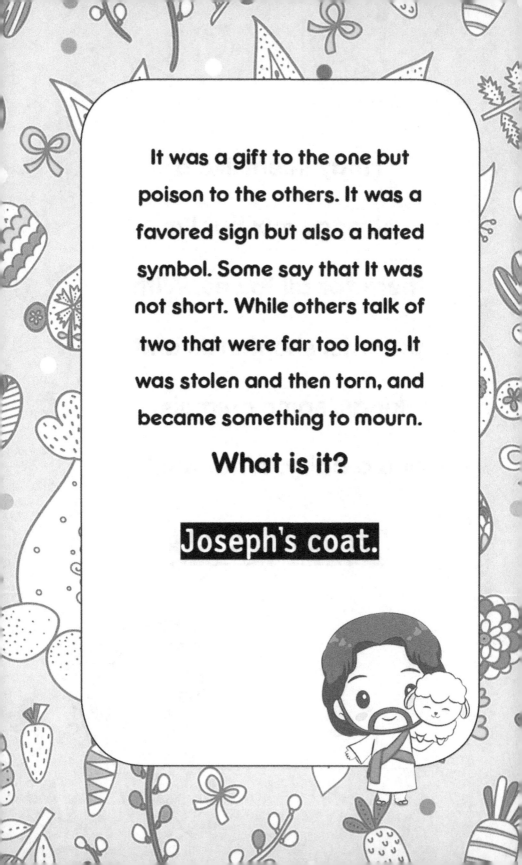

Instead of going to
Nineveh, I
decided to bail. Thrown
overboard while out to
sea, I was swallowed up
by a whale.

Who am I?

Jonah

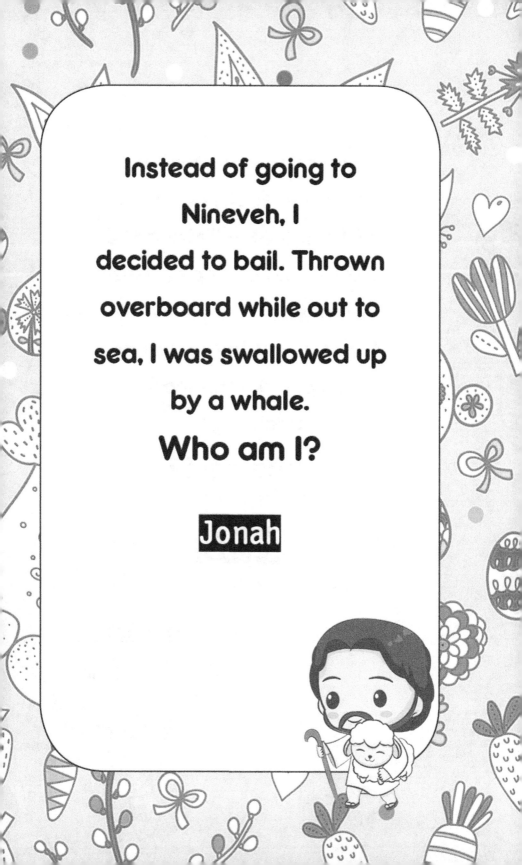

I loved God with all my heart and soul. I am a hero of faith that will stand the test of time as one of God's beloved. After all I went through, my faith and convictions remained unchanged.

Who am I?

Daniel

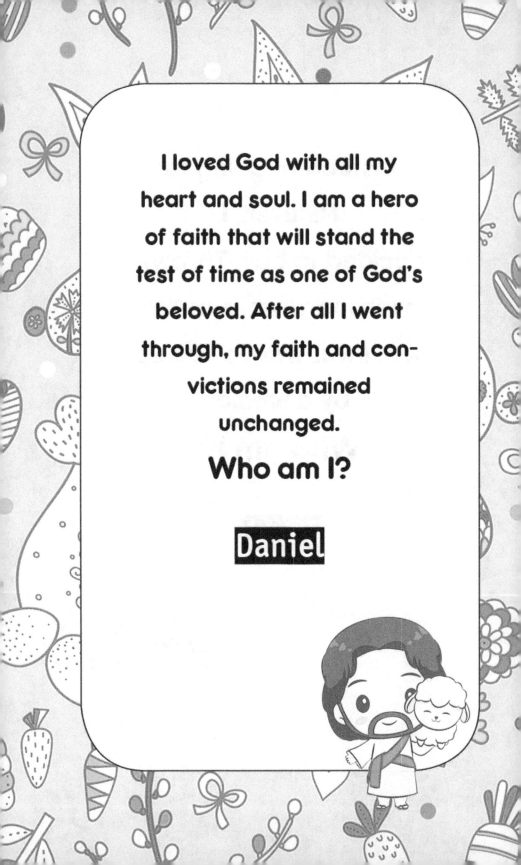

I am the book from the Bible from which many people derived the phrase 'Lamb for slaughter' from.

What book is this?

Isaiah

I am something you might read when you're sitting in a pew. I contain two testaments: one that's old and one that's new.

What am I?

The Bible

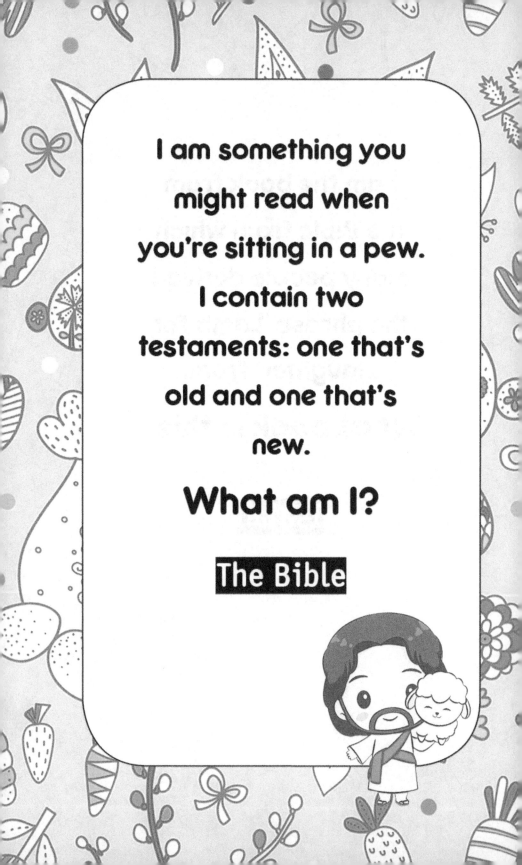

It was high in the sky but also firmly on the Earth. It brought cooperation for many but confusion for all. It was unmissable by the crowd yet overlooked by the One. It was the world's first true skyscraper and also its last.

What is it?

The Tower of Babel

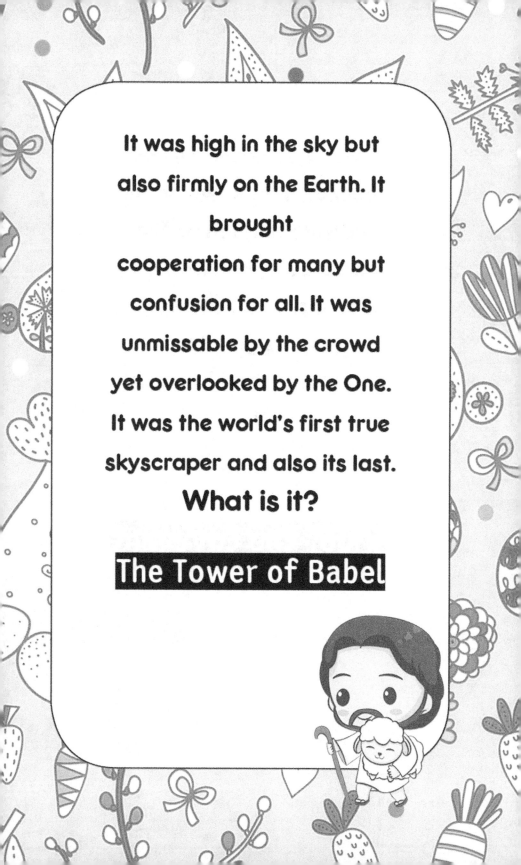

It can be carried but not touched. It has two on the outside and ten on the inside. Everyone wants to catch a sight of this but it's kept out of sight. It was lost and found; then found but now it's lost.

What is it?

Ark of the Covenant

I was known for my diverse skills as both a warrior and a writer of psalms. In my years as a ruler, I united the people of Israel, led them to victory in battle, conquered land, and paved the way for my son, Solomon, to build the Temple.

Who am I?

David

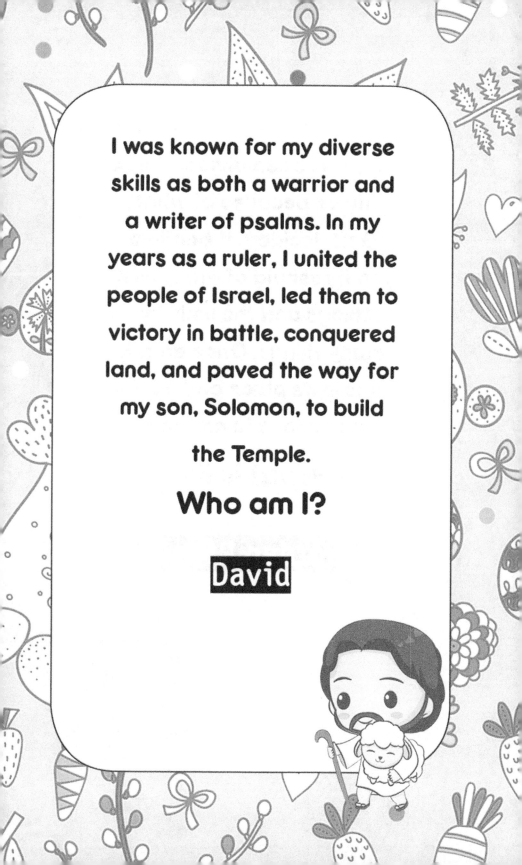

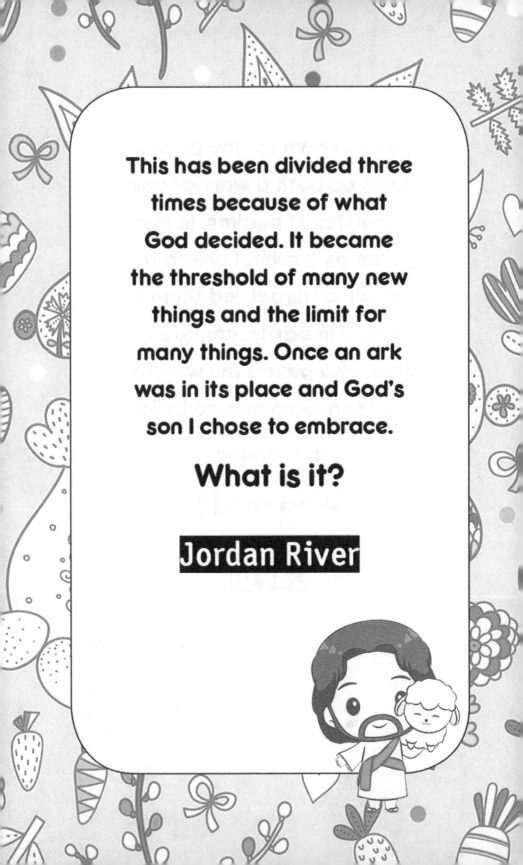

This has been divided three times because of what God decided. It became the threshold of many new things and the limit for many things. Once an ark was in its place and God's son I chose to embrace.

What is it?

Jordan River

When I was tasked with what seemed impossible, I didn't just refuse and frown. I marched the people round Jericho and the walls came tumbling down.
Who am I?

Joshua

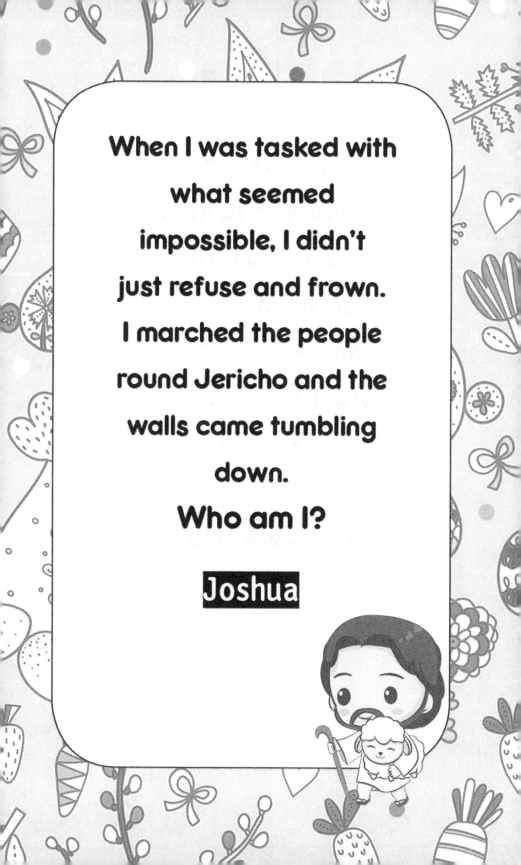

I am more than a double triangle. I intertwine both the external and internal dimensions of God, Israel, and the Torah. What am I?

The Star of David

I chose to climb a
sycamore tree to see
Jesus and invited him to
come to my house, even
though other people
sneered at me.

Who am I?

Zacchaeus

What is a shark's most favorite bible story?

Noah's shark.

Where did the

Bible's most

talkative people

live?

Babylon. (Babble on)

Which group of sharks do you typically find in heaven?

Angel sharks

What is the funny thing about forbidden fruits?

They create many jams.

Before Boaz

became married,

what kind of guy

was he?

Ruth-less

Why are atoms Catholic?

Because they have mass.

How do groups of angels greet each other?

Halo, halo, halo!

Who was the best female finance lady in the Bible?

Pharaoh's daughter. She went down to the bank of the Nile and drew out a little prophet

Who is the greatest babysitter mentioned in the Bible?

David — he rocked Goliath to a very deep sleep

Why wasn't Jesus born in the USA?

Because God couldn't find three wise men and a virgin.

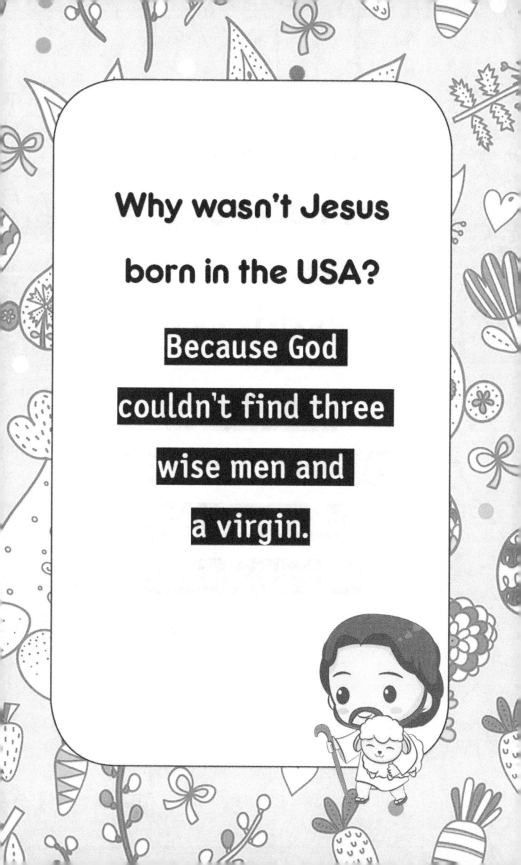

Did you hear about the 1-800 service they have for atheists now?

You dial the number and it rings and rings but nobody answers

Which part of the Bible won't you find a black man?

The Book of Job.

Who was the greatest female financier in the Bible?

Pharaoh's daughter. She went down to the bank of the Nile and drew out a little prophet.

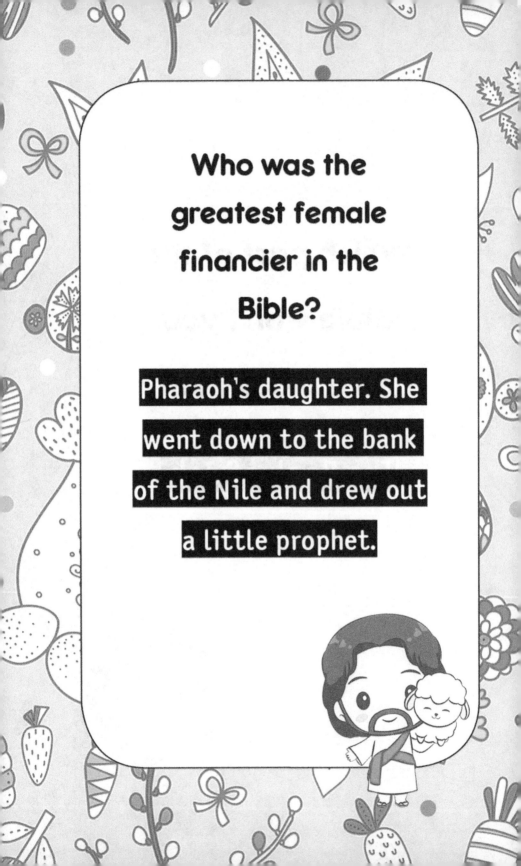

According to the Bible should men or women make coffee?

There's a whole book about it – He Brews.

How did Adam and Eve feel when expelled from the Garden of Eden?

They were really put out.

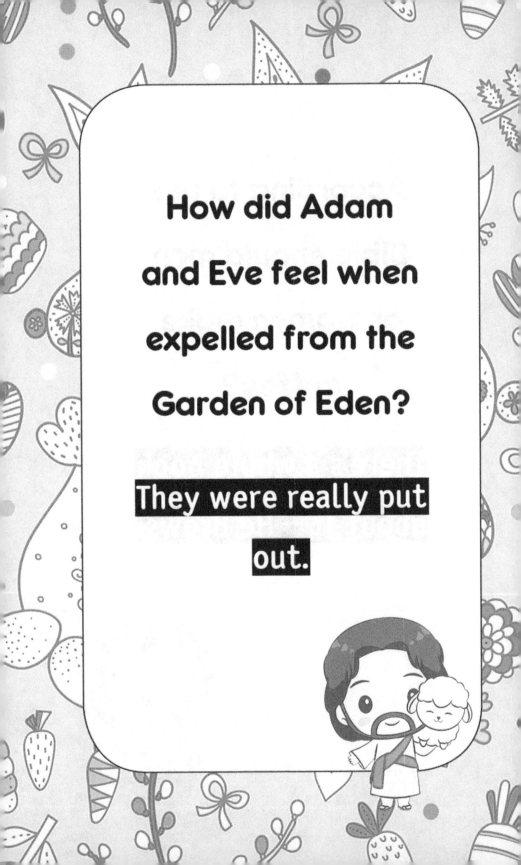

Where is the first mention of insurance in the Bible?

When Adam and Eve needed more coverage.

What is one of the first thing that Adam and Eve did after they were kicked out?

They really raised Cain.

Who is the shortest man mentioned in the Bible?

Bildad the Shuhite.

What do you call BATMAN skipping church?

Christian Bail

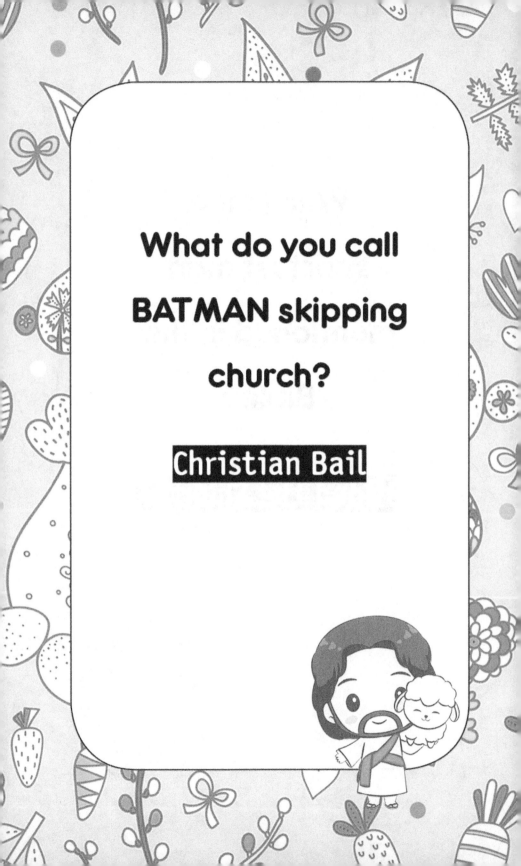

What was the last thing Noah said before he entered the Ark?

So long Fellers!

The ark was built in 3 stories and the top story had a window to let light in, but how did they get light to the bottom two stories?

They used floodlights.

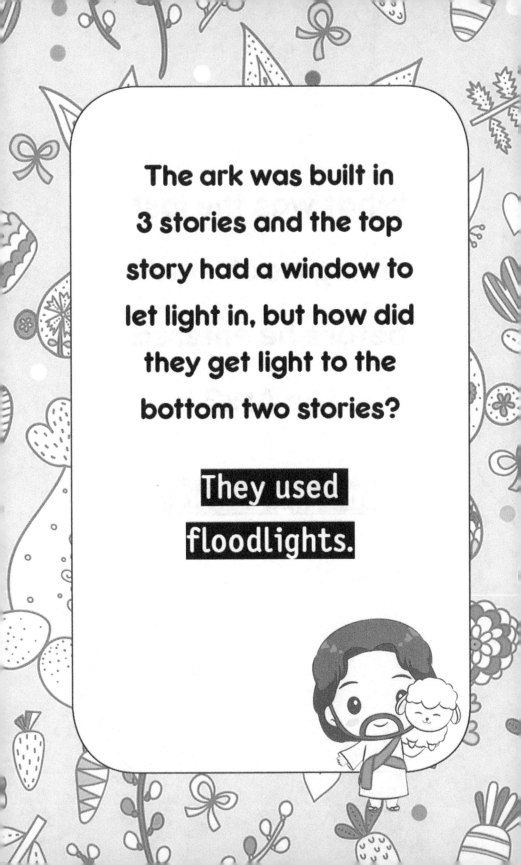

After the flood, how many people left the ark ahead of Noah?

Three. Because the Bible says that Noah went forth out of the ark.

Why won't we drink milk in the new world?

Because, at Armageddon, there will be udder destruction.

Why shouldn't Christians watch TV?

At the transfiguration, Jesus said, "Tell the vision to no one."

Who was the most

flagrant

lawbreaker

in the Bible?

Moses, because he
broke all 10
commandments at
once.

Who was the best mathematician in the Bible?

Moses. He wrote the book of Numbers.

Why do they say "Amen" at the end of a prayer instead of "Awomen"?

The same reason they sing Hymns instead of Hers!

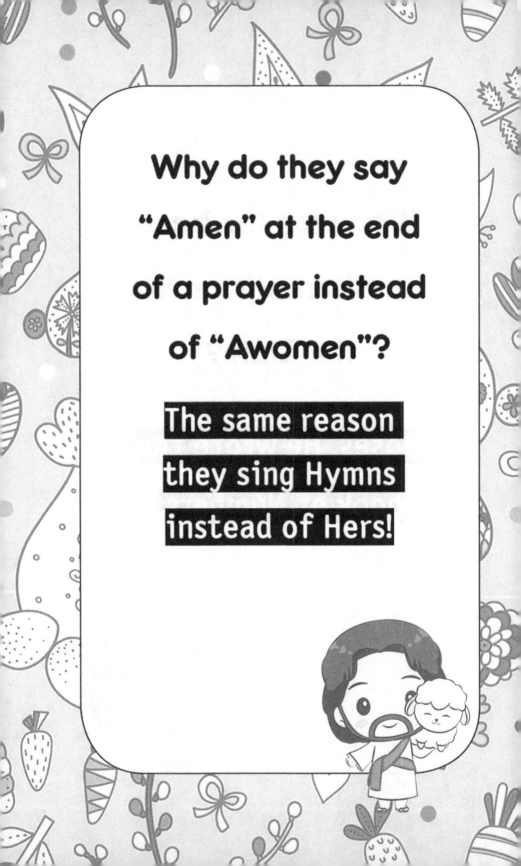

Why did Moses wander in the desert for 40 years?

Even then men wouldn't ask for directions.

What time of day was Adam created?

Just a little before Eve.

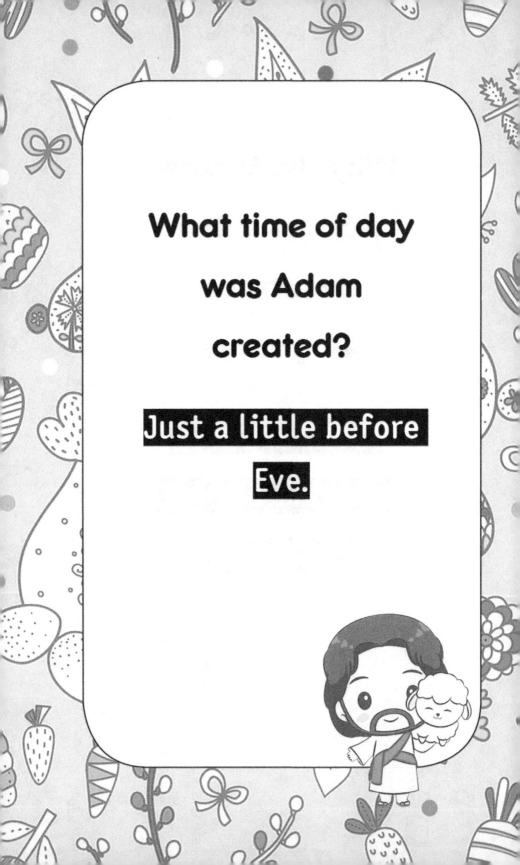

What do we have that Adam never had?

Ancestors.

Does God love everyone?

Yes, but He prefers "fruits of the spirit" to "religious nuts!"

What do you get if you cross a Jehovah's Witness and a Unitarian?

Someone who goes around knocking on doors for no apparent reason.

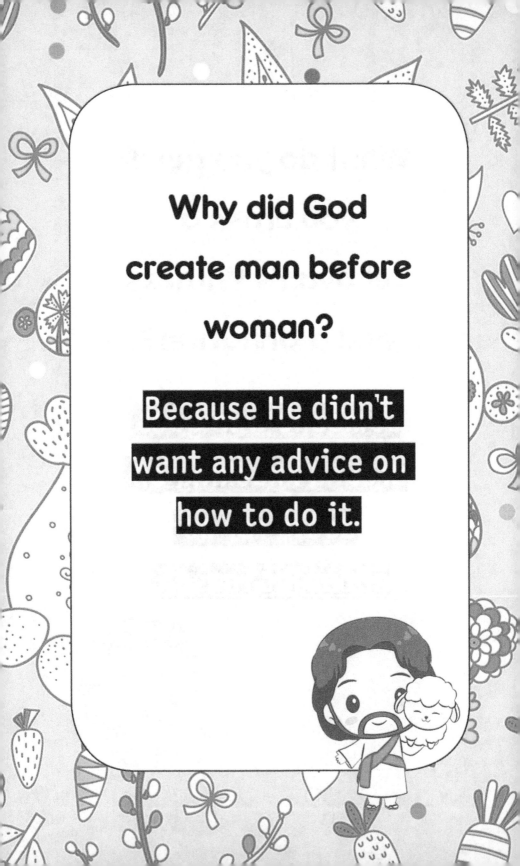

Which of the major prophets' books is the simplest to understand?

Ezekiel.

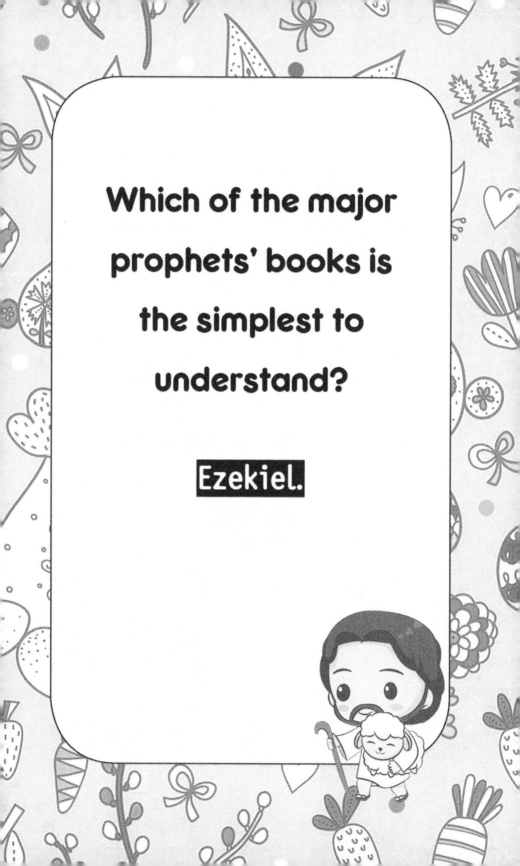

Which minor prophet has become well-known as a result of cookies?

Amos.

What do you call a prophet who also happens to be a chef?

Habakkuk.

What did Adam say to Eve as he handed her a garment?

"Either take it or leave it."

When Zachariah and Elizabeth disagreed, what did he do?

He delivered the silent treatment.

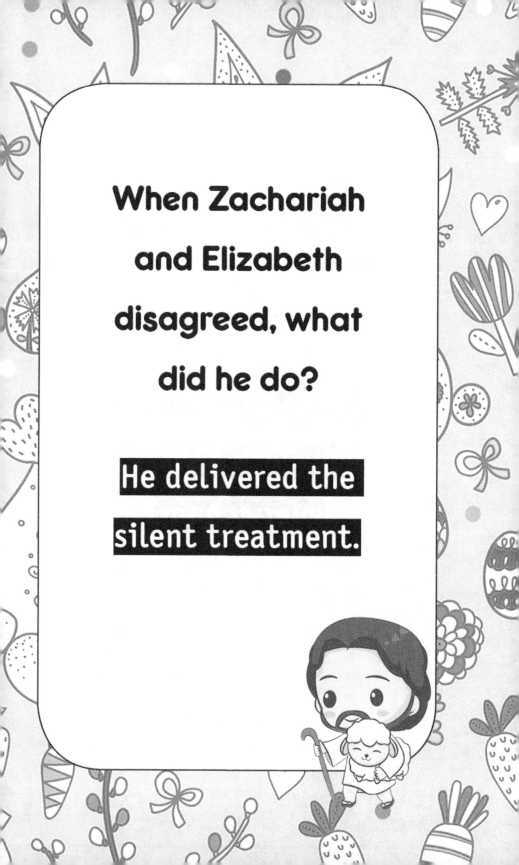

Why is it that Jesus cannot wear necklaces?

Because He is the one who breaks every chain.

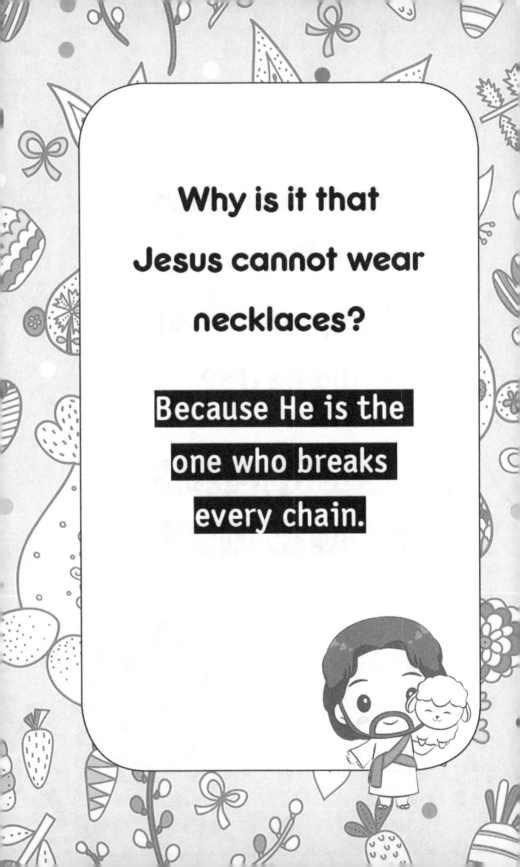

What is a
Christian's
favorite song to
listen to while
driving?

"Jesus, take the
steering wheel."

So, what did the Jew have to say to the Gentile?

"I wish you were Jewish."

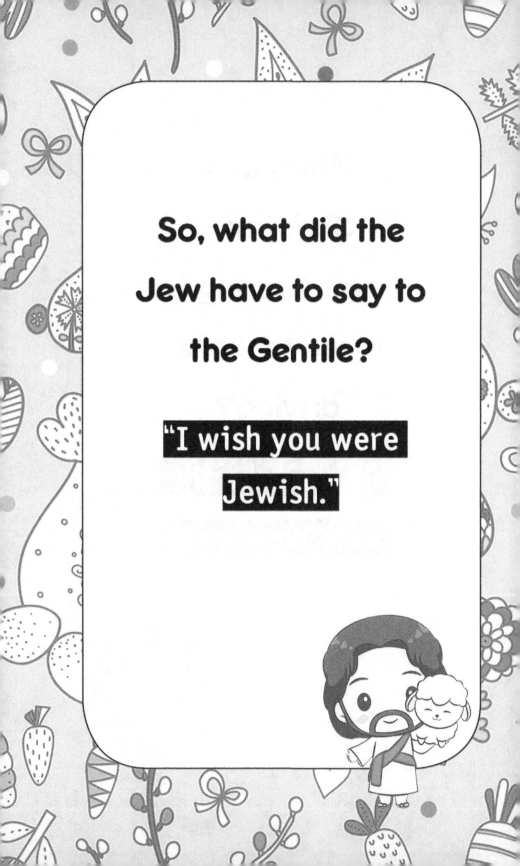

What time of day does Adam prefer?

Evening

What did Joseph tell Mary?

"Would you like to myrrh-y me?"

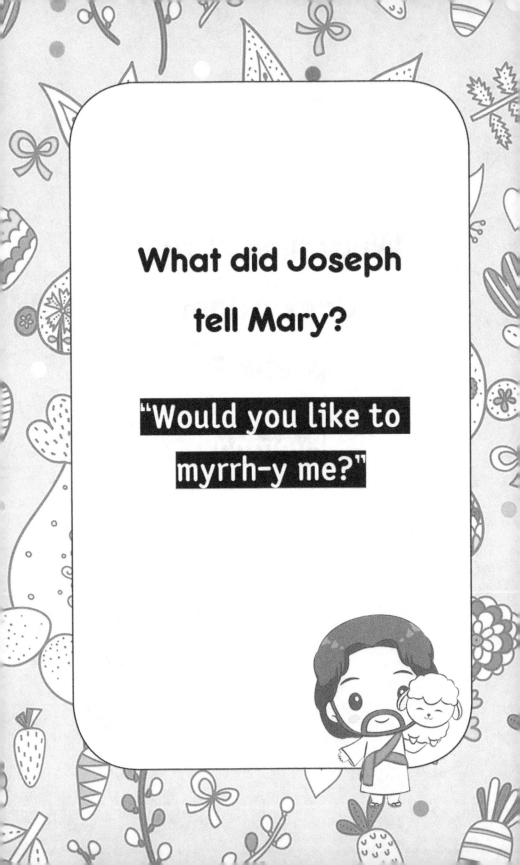

What did Sarai tell Abram while they were preparing Christmas dinner?

"The ham, Abram!"

When the disciples sneeze, what do they say?

Matthew!!!!

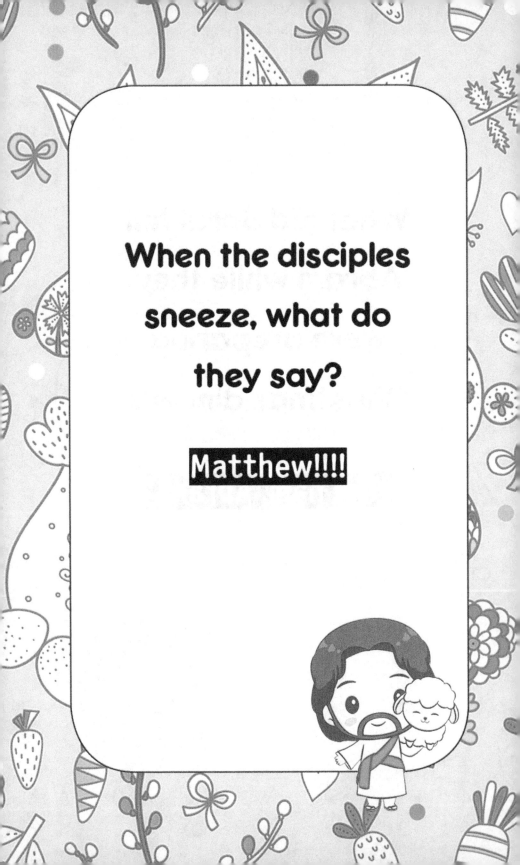

What did God have to say to Jesus?

I am your father, Jesus.

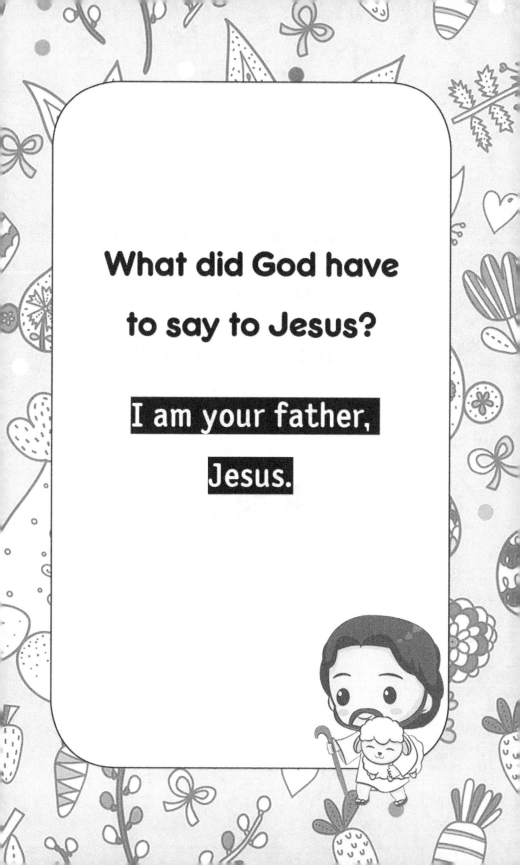

When Mary found
out she was
pregnant, what did
she say?

"Oh, my baby."

Which animal is Elisha's favourite?

She bears

What kind of car does Jesus drive?

He needs four-wheel drive because the clouds are bumpy.

Why were
the people
apprehensive
about worshipping
the Lord?

Because they
misheard us say
"warship."

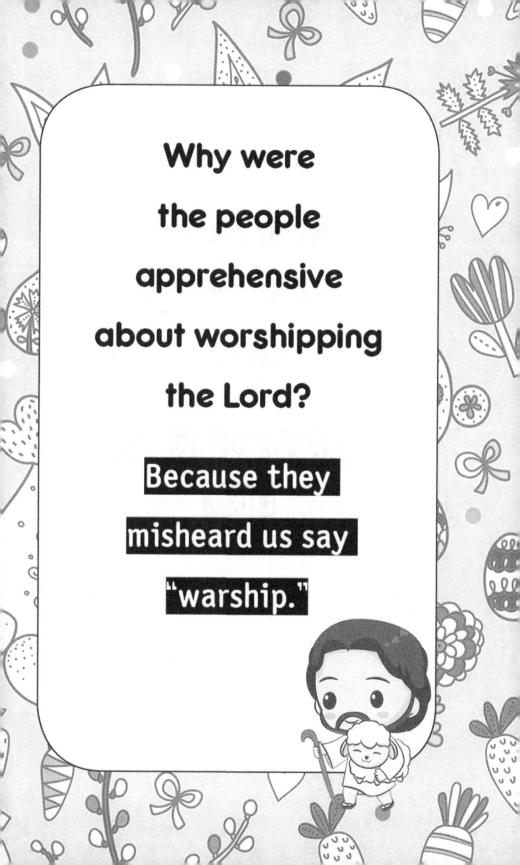

What did the doctor tell the child?

Allow me to take a Luke.

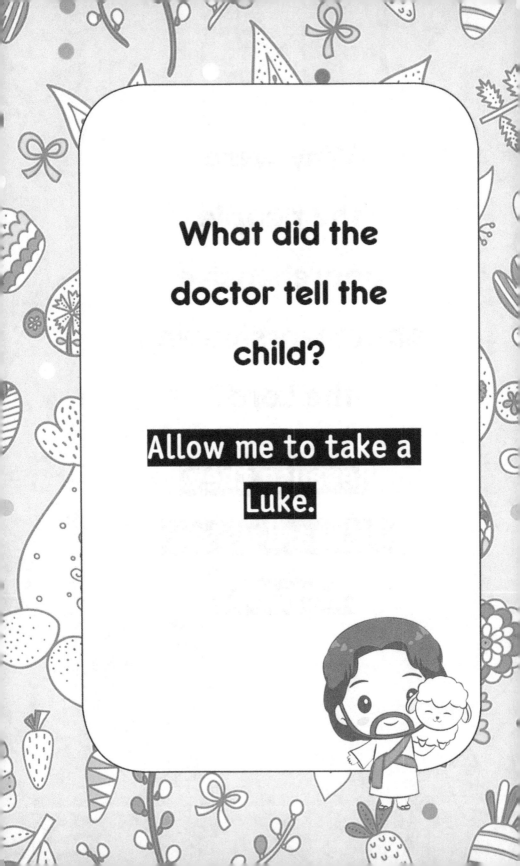

Where did Jesus
go to get
something to eat?

Mt. Olive

What is the court's favourite Bible book?

Judges

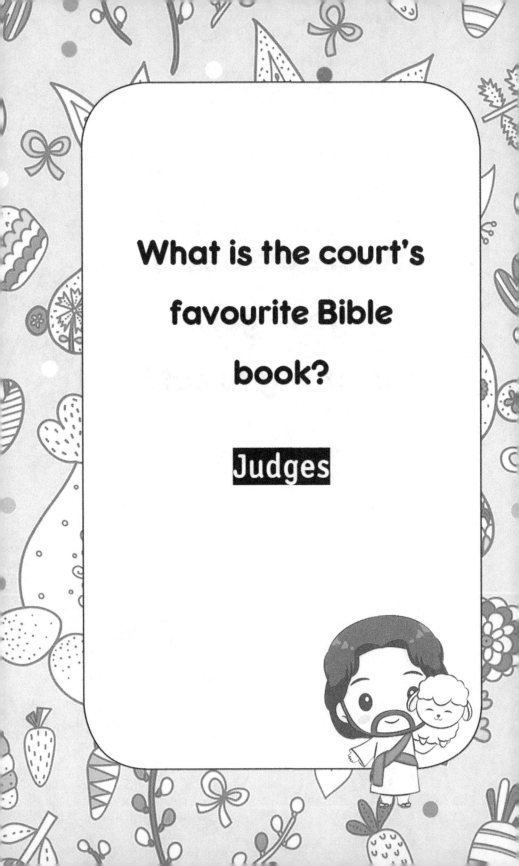

What kind of boats
do believers want
to travel on?

Worship and
discipleship

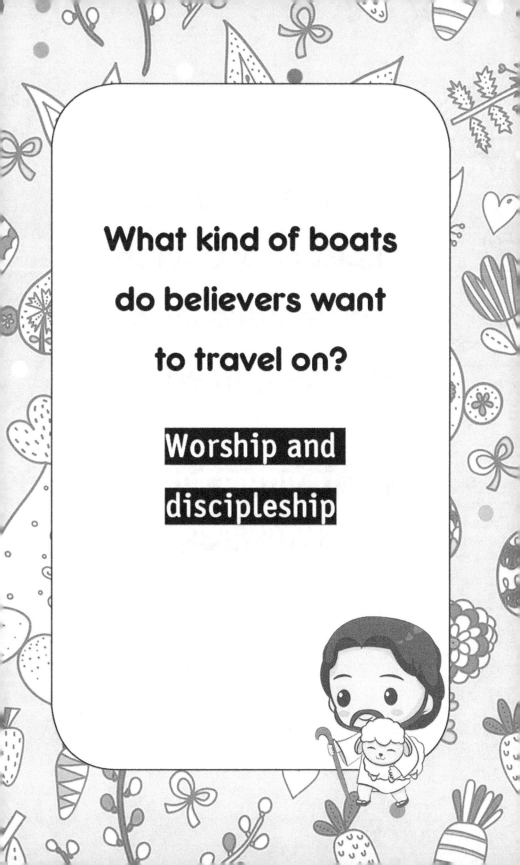

What does the
Episcopal Church
say in advance of
a large gathering?

"We're going to have
liturgy here."

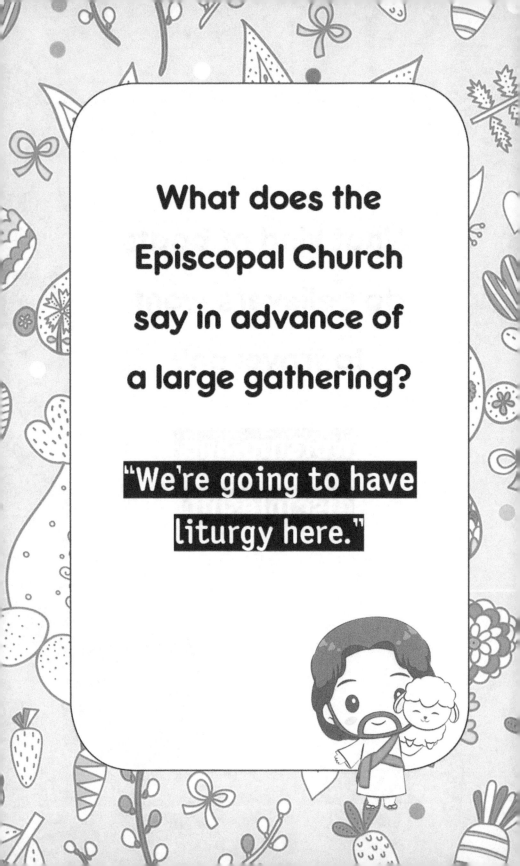

What kind of boats
do believers want
to travel on?

Worship and

discipleship

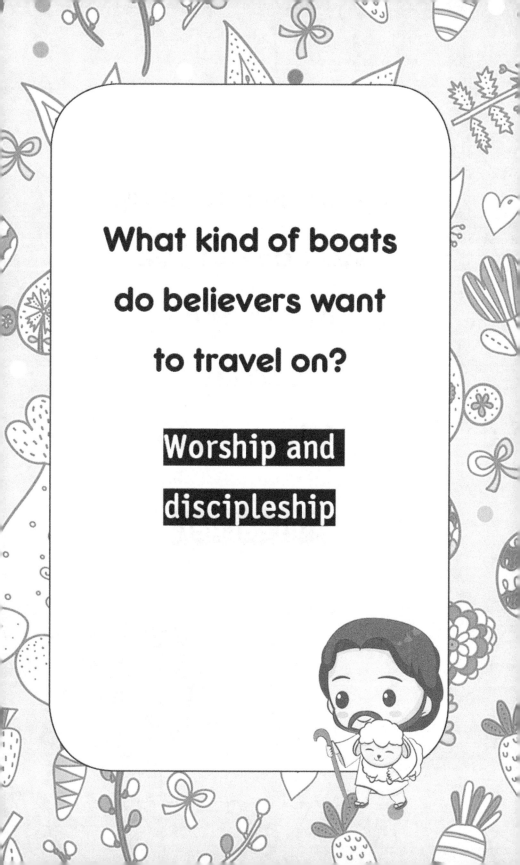

I've married many women but I've never been married.

Who am I?

A Preacher.

How do we know that cars are in the New Testament?

Because Jesus was a car-painter (carpenter)!

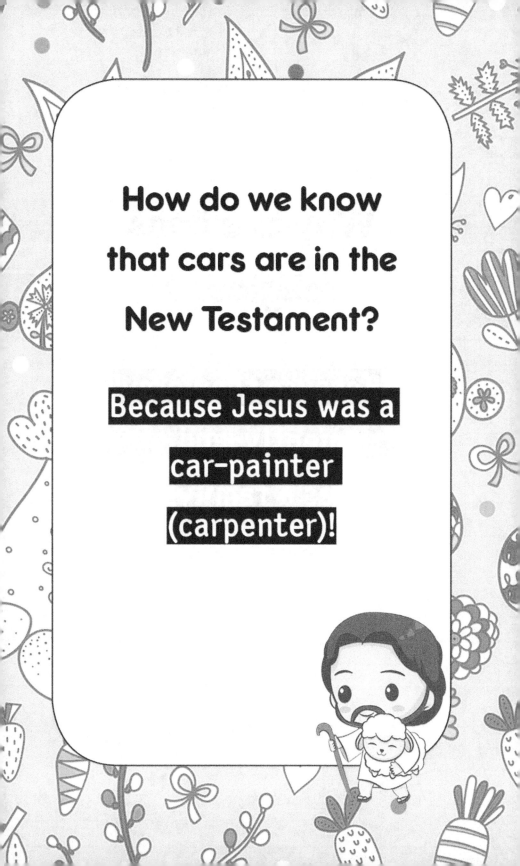

Why are lions religious?

Because they prey frequently, and prey as a family!

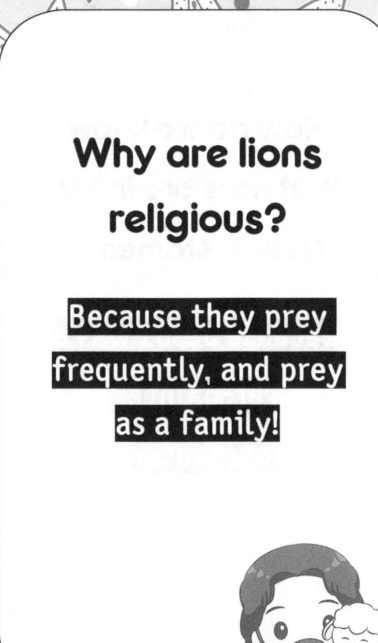

What do you call a Bible character who just pulled into church?

A parking Lot.

Why did Boaz hate lying?

Because he loved truth.

Made in the USA
Middletown, DE
12 November 2023

42447871R00091